Get the Message

Get the Message

Copyright © 2009 Aquila Media Productions
PO Box 2884
Addison, TX 75001

www.aquilamediaproductions.com

Portions of this book were originally published under the title *Understanding Your Life through Awareness* by Kathy Altaras.

Cover design, layout, and graphic additions: Dallas Drotz
Drotz Design

Library of Congress Cataloging-in-Publication Data

Altaras, Kathy

      Get the Message: What Your Car Is Trying to Tell You

Includes index

ISBN 978-0-9822705-4-7

LCCN 2009941382

Published in the United States of America

10 9 8 7 6 5 4 3 2 1

get the message

what your *car* is trying to tell *you*

Created by Nancy Tappe
Written by Kathy Altaras

AQUILA MEDIA PRODUCTIONS
ADDISON, TEXAS

acknowledgements

A book is the collective effort of many people. Thank you so very much to those friends who contributed their car challenges and road incidents for inclusion in these pages. Grateful appreciation also goes to those busy people who took time to read the manuscript and make suggestions. And finally, thanks to David who makes all things possible every single day.

contents

There are more things under heaven and earth, Horatio
Than are dreamt of in our philosophy.

Hamlet, I, iii

1 messages from your car

Not long ago I was driving north toward Los Angeles. At a juncture where two freeways come together, I noticed a car in distress several lanes to my right. Two young women in a small car had pulled off the freeway and were trying to rescue boxes and suitcases which had fallen from the cargo rack onto the freeway while they were driving. Several suitcases had burst, and items of clothing were buffeted about or trampled by the passing cars. Traffic was heavy; the girls looked panicked and miserable. A pick-up truck ahead of me had already stopped on the shoulder and was backing up to assist. Thoughts raced through my mind: gratitude that it wasn't me, sympathy for the girls and their plight, guilt for not having stopped, and regret that the driver probably had no clue that this event mirrored part of her personal life and that she would probably not get the message her car was giving her.

Our language is rich with metaphors linking driving with our everyday life. Everyone understands the metaphorical meaning of *the highway of life, driving in the fast lane, she's driving me crazy, being in the driver's seat, being wrapped around the axle, taking a back seat, or he really blew a gasket!* These figures of speech link situations in our daily lives with our car and its operation or malfunction in ways we can easily understand.

About twenty years ago, Nancy Tappe, a Southern California synesthete and psychic began to notice a pattern in the questions of many of her clients about their cars and car problems. They repeatedly asked her about the metaphysical meaning of their car accidents or car-related problems. And repeatedly, the information she received related to their everyday living, their body, or what was going on in their thought processes. She initiated a systematic research of this information, determining that our car does, indeed, act as a personal early warning system, relating to events in our lives, thoughts and emotions, or to our body. Nancy theorized that our car absorbs our unconscious thoughts and actions and then becomes a message center, mirroring those thoughts back to us. Many of the car parts relate to our body, but some represent how we think and work in the everyday world. The car symbolizes our body as it moves around from place to place — as we drive down the highway of life. It represents the transportation for our "self" that the body gives us. And if we take advantage of the information, our car acts as an early warning device, our own personal Doppler, indicating potential problems down the road.

In actuality, many pieces of machinery or equipment that we use constantly reflect and mirror us. We can take most mechanical or automatic machines that we are involved with (except a TV or computer, unless you know all the interior parts) and make it a message center. For a chef it might be the refrigerator, stove, or other piece of mechanical cooking equipment. Had they been aware, fifty or sixty years ago, women might have gotten their messages from their sewing machine, washing machine, or stove. A farmer could have gotten information from how his tractor drove and what broke or needed repair. Equipment or machinery that we use daily becomes an intimate part of us and absorbs our nature. But in today's world, the car is the mechanical aspect we use most frequently. The computer is also a message center, but it reflects another aspect of our life, and thus, the messages we receive from it are different.

In this book you will find the metaphor of the car as a message board or as a warning system explained in detail and instructions about how to apply the theory to your own life. The second half of Get the Message is a complete glossary referencing each part of the car, its relationship to your body or situation in everyday life, and finally, a series of questions you can ask yourself to help you fully understand how your car malfunction relates to you personally.

How the Car Works as a Message Center

The enormity of our unconscious mind does, indeed, work in ways we cannot begin to understand. Most brain researchers tell us that we consciously use somewhere between two and twelve percent of our brain's capacity. We are unable or unwilling to access most of the data stored there, and we do not even begin to tap into latent talents and abilities that are housed in the mind. In truth, we couldn't handle all the information even if we had complete access. Can you imagine having to plow daily through all your past events, feelings, senses, memories, thoughts, fears, and dreams – all the time? Of course not. But inadvertently, in our selective tuning out and repression of most of the conscious workings of our mind, we also close the door on sources of information that are available to use if we only knew how to access the data.

The unconscious constantly sends us data regarding what is happening to us. We send data back via our thoughts and deeds. The unconscious revises and processes it and then sends new data back. This process is constant and continuous. Early signals from the unconscious may come in the form of dreams. These signals can also be intuitive or just gut feelings about our health or our daily life. If the information from the unconscious deals more with our inner self, it will come through our dreams. The information may never get to the conscious mind because everything will occur in the unconscious mind.

But the information can come in other ways too. One of these is via your auto. If the information is about your actual body, the unconscious may begin to communicate to you via your automotive message center. The first hint will be a warning – a ping or a noise or some kind of indicator that trouble is coming. If you don't listen to it, the information may either repeat in a dream or in another physical manifestation in the car. Each repeat message will be a little louder, a little more dramatic. At first the repair will be minor – a ping or a little noise. If you are unaware or you don't get the message, the information may then go into your body itself as a minor ache or ailment. The message center processes the information continuously until you get it. Eventually, the need for a car repair or a repair in your body will be more serious. Ultimately, either the car or your body will break down.

The malfunction then is an indicator to you about what is going on in your life that needs adjustment or correction. Many of the most frequent and obvious car problems relate to your energy or your ability to move forward. For example, the battery symbolizes your charge on life, your energy and enthusiasm. Brakes refer to the need to "take a break." You are overworked and need to slow down. And within each mechanical system, the specific car parts related to that system can define the physical problems more concretely.

Fixing the car problem is an indicator to your unconscious that you are willing to correct the life problem as well. Failure to listen to the message (deal with the mechanical problem) results in a repeat message, more loudly and clearly down the road.

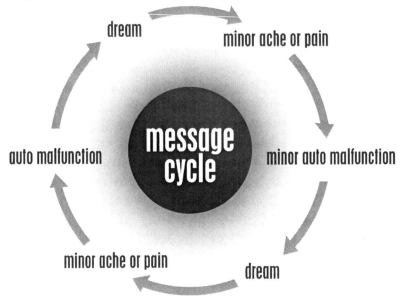

You can see a wonderful example of this cycle in the movie *Apollo 13*. Shortly before the launch of the ship, there are two short scenes illustrating this process. In one of them Jim and Marilyn Lovell are driving at night to a social function, and he has some minor trouble with the car stalling out. In another scene, she wakes up from a nightmare in which his space vehicle is badly damaged and chaos follows. To be sure, they are literary foreshadows. But they are also a clear representation of the cycle depicted in this book. We make no attempt to use this incident in any way beyond an illustration of how the cycle might work as a heads-up from the unconscious.

How to Get the Message

If you are seated in the driver's seat, you can divide the car into four basic sections. The right half of the car deals with your outer world or the right half of your body; the left half is your inner world (thoughts, dreams, fears, ambitions) or the left half of your body. The front of the car relates to the future; the back to the past. The driver and passenger areas refer to the present. Some parts of the car correlate to an entire system in the body. Others are more specific. Both the human body and the automobile are complex

left

inner world
*(dreams,
goals, fears,
ideals)*

right

outer world

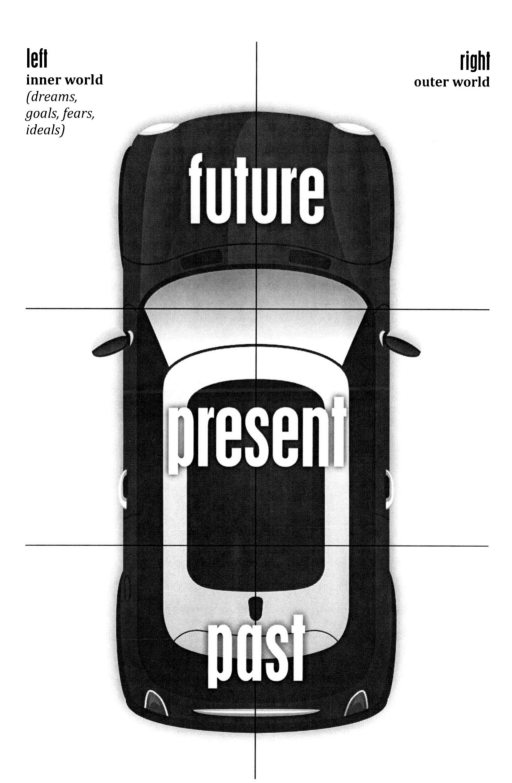

future

present

past

mechanisms consisting of entire systems working together. The glossary in the last half of this book will reference each car part and its corresponding section of your body, mind, or emotion.

The key is to become aware. And don't forget to read and think about this material with your inner skeptic at your side. Have fun with it. Continually ask yourself, is this information for me? What is going on in my life? What messages have I had from my car lately? Then check it out. Using this theory and reference book should become an on-going experimental process for you. Test it; practice it. How do you feel when you are in your car? What has happened to your car lately? How did you deal with it? What was going on in your life simultaneously, or in the case of the front of the car, in the near future? What were your challenges? How did you handle them? Become aware of your car when you are in it. At the same time, be aware of your body and yourself. If you have a problem with your car and a mechanic can't find the problem, then the burden is on you to figure out the message. Ask yourself what is not working in your life. If you can identify the challenge (i.e. get the message), the problem may never manifest in the car again.

car malfunction analysis

- Identify the section of the car where the malfunction took place.

- The left half of the car represents your inner world: fears, dreams, goals, ideals.

- The right half of the car represents your outer world, your daily life.

- Identify the section of the car representing timing in your life.

    - The front of the car represents the future.

    - The middle of the car represents the present.

    - The rear of the car represents your past.

- Use the glossary to determine the meaning of the car part and its malfunction. Determine whether the definition and description relates to your physical body, your stress level, or your everyday life.

- Use the questions to determine your personal message from this malfunction.

Be aware of one more thing. You can observe this phenomenon without ever admitting you believe or disbelieve the theory. Test it; try it. The magic of the entire process is that it is *your* unconscious giving *you* information about *you*, you life, your health, and your body or mind. *You* are the expert.

Once you understand the metaphor of the car as a message board, you will see that many of the meanings are literal and fairly simple. Brakes are about "taking a break" or "giving yourself a break." The brakes, tires, and battery all generally relate to your daily energy, you ability to move forward on the highway of life. Malfunctions are a reminder to you to get some extra rest or make small changes in a possibly hectic lifestyle.

Real-World Examples

As the manager of three offices for an international staffing company, I was running myself ragged travelling up to 200 miles a day between offices. I was working weekends: planning, strategizing, and training. I got up each business day at the crack of dawn and didn't return home in the evening until eight or nine o'clock. I could physically, mentally, and emotionally feel the exhaustion looming large on my horizon, much like one hears a train in the distance, but I ignored the signals.

I thought that if I could get each office operating correctly, the energy output would decrease, and I could simply enjoy my work; the rest would be a walk in the park. In truth, I was spinning plates. As soon as I got one office operationally profitable, my company gave me an additional failing office to turn around.

Finally, it all came to a head. One morning I woke up early to get a start on the day because a company auditor was auditing one of my offices located about an hour from my home. This audit was important because, although my staff had worked tirelessly to make certain we were 100% compliant, I knew their year-end bonuses would be affected if something went sideways. I went out to the garage and tried to start my car. Nothing. The engine didn't turn over. My husband wasn't in town, and I didn't have anyone to call, so I phoned my automobile club. I was freaking out when the tow truck driver arrived and couldn't diagnose the problem. His recommendation was to tow the car to my local dealership and have them diagnose the problem, which I knew from experience could take a good part of the day. As he started to prep my car for towing, I asked him to check the battery.

The driver courteously informed me that my kind of car actually had two batteries, one in the front and one in the back. He checked the front battery, and sure enough, it was dead. He then checked the back battery, and sure enough, it was also dead. He gave both batteries a charge, and within 15 minutes I was underway. I ended up making it to my office about ten minutes before the auditor arrived. I took the rest of the day off, drove to the auto dealership and purchased two new batteries. Once I got home, I called work and ended up taking the rest of the week off to rest too.

The narrator of this event says, "After that experience, I listened and responded to my body. I realized what a toll my work life had taken on my energy. When I felt my energy losing its charge, I took some time off to re-energize. It was a wonderful lesson."

Here is another one:

I was on my way to the airport (nearly an hour away) and was close to my destination. My car died at a stoplight. Luckily a couple of good Samaritans pushed me into a hotel parking lot. I called a tow truck and had my car towed to my mechanic's shop. I caught a shuttle to the airport and proceeded to go on my business trip.

When I spoke to the mechanic, he said that the transmission was completely gone. The repair bill would be in the thousands. I didn't know what to do. I had just leased both my homes in long-term rentals. I had no idea where I was going to move or how I would get there. My work takes me places where I rent a car or use public transportation.

When I got back home several weeks later, I rented a car for several months. Even if I had replaced the transmission, my car was so old that it would probably need something again soon. I still haven't dealt with the car.

The narrator of this event says, "I don't know why this car thing happened. I already knew my life was falling apart. The transmission referred to my emotions and my ability to move forward smoothly and automatically. I just didn't know what changes to make. I had nowhere to live, no place to work, and no specific plans. I didn't fear the changes at all. I had enough money to live, and I trusted that the right doors would open. But I also didn't deal with the problem, pay for, or get rid of the car, and move on. I still am not settled with my life."

2 routine maintenance and repair

O ne of the advantages of knowing about how the auto functions as a message center for your body and your thoughts in the everyday world is that you can be proactive in heading off problems. Careful, periodic maintenance on your car keeps it functioning smoothly and prolongs its life. So, too, does methodical and regular maintenance on your body. When you take the car in for a tune-up, take time to contemplate your health and your ability to go through your day with plenty of energy. Do you need a dietary change? Is it time to get back on an exercise program? Should you have a check-up or take care of those health issues you have been putting off? Have you had your yearly check-up? How has your health been during the last year? What can you do to improve your health and energy level for the year ahead? Ask yourself what changes you can make that will give you a new lease on life or a fresh, new beginning. What can you do to energize yourself for the weeks ahead?

It is important to follow a regular routine of car and body maintenance. Failure to do this can create more frequent problems in both places. It is also practical to take care of problems while they are small rather than waiting for them to become dramatic, expensive, and time-consuming. As always, your car will warn you when your energy is low or when you need to address some issue in your body or in your daily life. Keep your message center clear; it's a direct line from your unconscious.

As we continue to evolve as a species, our bodies are becoming more sensitive and fine-tuned. We see this clearly by the way our diets have changed in the last twenty years, away from heavy meat, potatoes and gravy-based meals three times daily to more emphasis on grains, fruits, and vegetables. Culturally, we ourselves are aware of the importance of a lighter, more moderate diet as a lifestyle. Our cars have also become more refined to parallel this evolution in ourselves. We no longer use leaded fuel, and now, each time we buy gasoline, we even have several choices of octane to meet the specialized needs of our cars.

Even the inner mechanisms of the cars themselves have become refined. Some elements within the car have changed from one part to an entire system of parts. For example, the old "carburetor" has become the "fuel injection system," a series of interconnected parts working together to move fuel and air through the system to create energy. We see further reflection of this evolutionary refinement with the increase in hybrid cars, which reflects our need to utilize and conserve our own energy more consciously, more economically, and more efficiently. If you drive a hybrid, you are becoming more aware of using your energy more consciously, effectively, and efficiently. This may relate to your physical body, your money, or both.

Fuel enables your vehicle to run – to move forward. Many of us put the cheapest fuel in our cars all the time. We eat the same way —the fastest, most convenient food possible. If that's what we do to our car, then we are likely to do the same to our body. If you want quality out of your car or body, you need to put quality in. The body is a print-out of your thoughts and your living processes, reflective of what you do and think, as well as how you act. Adding gasoline to the car provides you with frequent opportunities to take a moment to check your diet. Are you putting in the right nutrients for the best of your body? Do you use moderation with the temptations of living in a "fast-food nation?" Is it time to make the necessary refinements regarding your diet to enable you to allow your digestive system to run more smoothly? Being aware of the adjustments in your system and becoming more sensitive to the messages from your subconscious will allow you to follow life's highway smoothly both in the car and in the body.

Routine Maintenance

Most automotive tune-ups today focus on simple wear and tear. Many people are diligent about replacing oil and filters regularly. These simple replacements represent good energy and balance in the body. Replacing them routinely is a good step forward on keeping the car moving efficiently and preventing a breakdown in the system. Clogged filters and dirty oil are the same as having a toxic body, flu, colds, or a virus. It may not be enough to get you down, but it definitely keeps you from running at peak performance. In the case of your car or body, an ounce of prevention is worth a pound of cure.

Battery

The battery is the most important message center in the car. It symbolizes your metabolism and indicates how energy moves through your body. It can also relate to the reproductive system or your electrolytes. The battery symbolizes your "charge" on life. A dead battery indicates that you are exhausted physically, mentally, or emotionally. The charge is gone. If possible, take a day off for rest and relaxation. It usually isn't a long-term problem. And there is an upside. A dead battery demands an immediate fix in the car, and resting a day or two will revitalize the body. Both problems can be relatively quick fixes.

A Real-World Example

Within six weeks both my husband and I had incidents involving our battery cables. In his case we were out shopping. When we got out to the parking lot, the car was dead. We had to phone AAA for assistance. The tow truck driver diagnosed the problem as a loose battery cable. He reconnected it securely, and we were on our way. Six weeks later I intended to leave home for an appointment, but when I got in the car, it was dead. A few hours later my husband (intending to take the battery out and buy a new one), discovered that the battery cables were corroded. He got out some sand-paper and cleaned them up. The car started just fine. He subsequently had both batteries checked; both were fine. It was just the cables both times.

The narrator of this event says, "Clearly the message was for both of us. We didn't take the time to figure it out the first time, so it came around again. We used the glossary and interpreted the meaning of battery cables as an opportunity to revitalize our goals for the future. As we did so, we realized that we hadn't done so for many years. We still had goals, but some of our life circumstances had changed. In his case his vision of the future had gotten loose. Perhaps he had 'disconnected' when he didn't feel he had accomplished his dream. In my case the message seemed to indicate that some of my goal-setting processes were rusty or toxic. We did some talking and thinking. We realized that we didn't have to replace our goals, just clean them up a bit or refine things."

Brakes

Brakes comprise a whole system with many parts. There are front and rear brakes, brake drums, pads, boosters, shoes, and brake fluid. All of them relate to your feet, your immune system, or your sense of discipline and self-control. They ask you to acknowledge how you stop and take a break. Trouble in this area means you are over-worked, and you need to slow down. Front brakes may relate to your toes; rear brakes (and brake pads) refer to the heels or your Achilles heel or blisters. The brake booster refers to eating or drinking something to keep going (usually a high calorie sugar substance). Brake drums refer to the joints, especially hips or knees. Brake fluid relates to the blood flow and circulation to the feet. Brake shoes refer to your feet. Anti-lock brakes mirror your thinking processes and your ability to concentrate clearly. Brake failure means that you have lost your ability to know when to slow down. You are out of control. Replacing your brakes indicates your willingness to readjust your timing and pace yourself more appropriately for your body and mind.

A Real-World Example

The brakes on our car started making a really loud grinding sound. We took the car in, hoping it would be just pads or shoes. Not even close. We had to replace the whole brake system. Even after we got them fixed, there was still a problem. The right front brake still made noise. I took the car in again; they made a minor adjustment, and then everything was fine.

The narrator of this event remembers, "While the brake stuff was happening, we were both tremendously busy. We had work plus a bunch of concerts at night. We were really tired. I'm sure the message was to slow down and stop the constant activities. I knew for myself that the pace was just too hectic."

Tires

Tires relate to your hands and feet. They reflect your energy and your balance, or they mirror your sense of being grounded. A flat tire means you are losing energy; it's time to rest up. Front tires deal with the future; rear tires deal with the past. A blow-out means you have lost all your energy. Tires with no tread indicate that you are stressed in life. You don't have a good grip on your life at the present time. Your understanding or patience has worn down. Needing tire chains means that you need a better grip on life.

pings and dings

Pings, dings, and minor problems on the surface of your car relate to your self-esteem. They are sore spots, reflections of the frustrations that everybody experiences. Most drivers don't want to go to the trouble and expense of paying someone else to smooth them out. They are the physical or emotional scars that occur in life. They can also be surface injuries that have not healed.

3 collision!

Nothing in life is as unsettling as a traffic accident. Culturally, we are trained that accidents are bad. To be sure, they are dramatic and usually emotional. But the important thing to remember is that accidents in themselves are not bad. They definitely are a wake-up call from your message board. But they can also bring a release of energy that, once dealt with, enables you to move forward more positively as long as you do the necessary repair work.

Some accidents, however, go beyond just "unsettling." The potential for serious injury, damage to someone else, and even death are part of driving, as they are part of life. Are they still messages from your unconscious? Yes, indeed. They are serious and sometimes life-altering indicators that changes must be made.

An auto accident is a warning that you are off in the outer world, and it is usually the end of a long line of messages you have not noticed or heeded. It means you are not paying attention to something. You are on a possible collision course with something in your life. If it occurs on the front of the car, it can refer to a coming confrontation or a shocking experience. It may be a warning of careless actions. Perhaps you are running into someone else's beliefs or behavior.

A collision from the rear indicates something you didn't resolve from the past. Perhaps something from your past is going to resurface in your life, causing you trouble, heartache, or grief. You may have unfinished business from the past. However, there can be some benefits from this. Being rear-ended moves you into correct timing with your life and enables you to have the opportunity to clean up the past.

Interpreting the messages from your accident involves the same process as repairing a malfunctioning car part. Refer to the glossary to find out the meaning of each damaged part. Apply that definition and description to yourself, your body, or your life. See if you can find out what part of your life the message relates to. What car parts have to be repaired or replaced? What questions should you ask yourself to help you find the correlation?

The next step is to see who was at fault in the accident. Were police (authority figures) involved? Who will pay the damages? Do you carry insurance to protect yourself in these kinds of situations? Are you able to carry the burden of any extra bills not covered by insurance yourself? Do you have to do the leg work, i.e. have the car towed, find a body shop, or locate an insurance-approved mechanic? Is someone else at fault? If so, then you will have to share the burden of the message, but you don't have to pay the price. In this case it will be much easier for you to be objective as you work through the analysis.

What does it mean if your car is totaled? Obviously, it's a big message. This accident requires you to look at the big picture of your life. It also forces you to accept responsibility for what is going on in your life. What were you doing when the accident happened? Were you going to or from work or driving for a work-related purpose? If so, then the message is possibly about your job. Were you and a friend or relative arguing, or were you coming or going from something involving a relationship? If so, evaluate that whole relationship. What changes are needed in your life that you have been ignoring?

Once again, use the glossary. Apply the meanings of the car parts that were damaged or destroyed. How do those messages speak to you? What needs to be addressed or changed?

✸ auto accident analysis

- Identify the section of the car where the malfunction took place.

- The left half of the car represents your inner world: fears, dreams, goals, ideals.

- The right half of the car represents your outer world, your daily life.

- Identify the section of the car representing timing in your life.
  - The front of the car represents the future.
  - The middle of the car represents the present.
  - The rear of the car represents your past.

- Determine whether authorities (police) were part of the experience.

- Determine who bears most of the responsibility: were you responsible for the accident, did you get a ticket, who will pay the bill, did you have insurance?

- Use the glossary to determine the meaning of the car part and its malfunction. Determine whether the definition and description relates to your physical body, your stress level, or your everyday life.

- Use the questions to determine your personal message from the damaged auto parts.

If you are involved in an accident where it is not your car and you are only a passenger, then your involvement with the message board is lessened, and you have greater objectivity. However, you were there. You have residual responsibility. Again, you will be more objective in your analysis than if you were driving in your own car. You can ask yourself, if it had been my car, what would this event have meant to me? Don't assume that you are completely free from the impact of the message. Just know that the impact is lessened.

Whatever kind of accident you were involved in, it may take some effort and practice to work out the meaning. Accidents are dramatic and emotional. It is much more difficult to maintain your objectivity during an analysis from a traffic accident than from a malfunction. But the potential for positive change is significant.

A Real-World Example

I was trying to turn left across two lanes of traffic. I didn't have excellent vision, but a woman driver gestured to me that I could pull out in front of her. As I pulled beyond her, I was broadsided by a pickup truck. I barely remember any of it. Later I was not able to get my car door open and get out of the car. I sat there in a daze for a long time. Eventually the other driver came over and was able to get the door open. The police came. I know the other driver was speeding, but I got the ticket. Everything from the driver side forward was crushed. The insurance company declared the car a total loss. I had a lump above my left knee for months but nothing else.

The narrator of this event says, "I knew that having my car totaled meant that the message was significant. And I knew that the left side of the car represented my inner self, my thoughts, goals, dreams, and ideals. So I clearly needed to do some inner work. The door, fenders, and even the firewall were crushed or destroyed. I applied the meanings of those parts. When the accident happened, I was on my way to a counseling session for weight loss. I had (sadly) pulled into a fast food place to get a snack before I went in. The meanings of the car parts seemed to relate to my self-esteem, weight loss program goals, and the blocks I was experiencing during the therapy. Since I got the ticket, I realized that I had to assume full responsibility for the incident. A couple of years later I got a melanoma on my left knee and had it successfully removed. I think I didn't get the full impact of the message from the auto accident. The next time the message came around was more serious, but I dealt with it."

Another person reports an incident where she rear-ended the car in front of her:

> I was on the freeway in the middle lane of four lanes of traffic. There had been occasional slowdowns, and traffic would speed up again. During one of the slowdowns, I applied the brakes and then noticed that traffic had begun to move forward again. I accelerated but saw the car in front of me slow down. I took my foot off the accelerator. Too late, I realized that it had stopped completely. I rear-ended it. My front end was crushed, more on the right side than the left and to the extent that the front right passenger door wouldn't open at all. My left hand and wrist were injured.

The narrator of this event says, "I should have seen this coming. I had had a dream a few weeks earlier about my car being sent to the crusher. I didn't pay any attention. According to the glossary the front of the car represents the future, and the right side is the outer world. I see it as getting a new mental perspective on my future. The car was declared a total loss. I got my dream car as a result. But my fingers still hurt. I'm not sure how long the healing will take."

Another driver tells the story of a freak incident that can happen in today's world:

I was with my boyfriend. We were in my car driving in the fast lane on the freeway. He was tired and had reclined his seat all the way so he could get some rest. All of a sudden a surfboard from an SUV in another lane got loose and flew off the top of that car. It flew straight at us and broke through the passenger side front window, stopping within one inch of my boyfriend's face. Had he not been fully reclined, he would have been disfigured or possibly killed.

The narrator of this event says, "We were both so grateful that this accident wasn't much worse. As it was, it scared both of us completely. In a few weeks we decided to get married, kind of spur of the moment. But it didn't last long at all. I know that the front windshield is the view of the future. I guess it's possible that the meaning for him was about getting married in haste. I mean we had hardly gotten over the accident before we got married."

4 cars in your dreams

Your car sends you messages, even in your dreams. The unconscious continually transmits data regarding what is happening to you. You send data back via your thoughts and deeds. The unconscious revises and processes that information and then sends new data back. This process is constant and continuous, whether you are aware of it or not and whether you believe in it or not. Early signals from the unconscious may come in the form of dreams. These dreams work together with your car or other machinery you use to keep you informed and, occasionally, warned, about your own living processes. It is not necessary to be a dream interpreter to get information from your own car dreams. Simply remembering the car dream and applying the meaning from the glossary can provide you with valuable information.

Car parts have the same significance in your dreams as they do in your actual car itself, especially in those dreams that occur immediately before you wake up. The "story" of the dream isn't very important. Again, remember, you don't have to know how to analyze dreams to access car information. It is, however, vital to remember the dream or write it down as soon as possible to facilitate the car message. Quite often, if you can work with the information that comes in dream form, the problem will never materialize in the actual car itself. The messages from the car in your dreams act as a heads-up, announcing potential challenges and problems. Awareness of this process will make "getting the message" much easier.

how to interpret car information from your dreams

- Pay attention to what the vehicle is doing in the dream and to what is going on in the environment. Is the environment clear or murky? How do you feel in the environment of this dream? Are you comfortable or uncomfortable?

- Notice where you are in the car. Are you the driver or a passenger? Are you "in the driver's seat," or is someone else in control? Do you have the car under control? Are you comfortable where you are?

- Observe the road. Is it straight, curvy, or bumpy? Do you have clear vision of the road ahead? Are you moving forward? All these can be indicators of how you are moving through a situation in your life.

- Watch how you are driving – recklessly, carelessly, safely, or cautiously. Are you driving yourself too hard? Are you paying attention to where you are going? Are you moving forward or backward?

- See if the car is functioning properly. Are there any malfunctions?

- Note the end of the dream. Is there a satisfactory conclusion? Did you have to take action to get things to work out okay? Do you need to check out some part of your physical vehicle, or (after checking the glossary) do you need to keep an eye on some part of your physical body?

- Document the date of the dream. If this event or something like it actually happens, note the time lapse. This can be a valuable timing device from your mind to your daily life.

Practice makes perfect. As you work with this personal system of communication, you may be amazed about the accuracy and applicability of information from your own message center. You can also become aware of the many advantages there are in utilizing your own messages to steer clear of trouble ahead.

Sample Dreams

Sample #1

I was driving up a very curvy mountain. As I got to one curve, I didn't make the curve and my left front wheel was hanging over the cliff. I got out of the car (uncharacteristic of me) and looked at the tire. It was hanging like a bag over the cliff. I got back in the car, put it in reverse, and backed it back on the road. I got out, looked at the tire, and it was perfectly normal. I woke up.

The dreamer says, "I dreamed this very vividly right before I woke up. I knew that the tires represented balance and grounding. In the dream, I backed up the car and things were all right. So I got up, cancelled my appointments for the morning and slept until noon. When I got up later, I was fine. I appreciated the dream as an indicator that I was overtired."

Sample #2

I drove up a slight hill and parked my vehicle on the left curb. I got out of the car and started to walk to my destination. But I noticed that the car rolled backward down the hill and ran into a pick-up truck. I was shocked. It didn't seem to do any damage to the pick-up. I still was concerned. Then it started to roll completely back down the hill, and it ended up running into a pre-school or daycare. I went outside and saw some people outside. I called their attention to the accident, but none of them seemed to care.

The dreamer says, "Two weeks after I had this dream, I was notified at work that a client had issued a formal complaint against me regarding something I had done right before vacation. My superiors did not seem concerned at all. Over a two-month period, the client progressed through the employer's complaint system; each time my superiors followed the system and denied any wrong-doing on my part. I was alarmed at how the system worked since I had never gone through it during my entire 14 years of employment. After awhile, the matter just died away."

In the chart below you will find some basic car symbolism that can commonly appear in your dreams. And although dream symbolism is entirely unique to each individual, you can see if this information fits your dreams as messages from your unconscious self to your life.

at a glance

symbol in dream	Interpretation
auto accident	Not paying attention to something. On a collision course with something in your life. It can represent a coming confrontation or a shocking experience. Running into someone else's beliefs or behavior. May be a warning of careless actions. A collision from the rear indicates something you didn't resolve from the past.
backing up	Losing ground or backing out of a situation. Re-evaluating or going back over something in your mind, or the need to re-evaluate a situation happening in your life.
blowing the horn	If you are the driver and are blowing the horn, you are showing off, i.e. tooting your own horn. But it could also be warning you or someone else to be careful.

brakes defective, can't stop the car	You don't know how to stop. If you are stomping on the brake or shifting down, you are having to work extra hard or do more things to slow down. Your automatic ability to slow down when you need to isn't functioning.
bumpy road	Environmental things that you need to pay attention to. Slow down: drive carefully. Or things ahead of you are problematic, causing you to go slower or more carefully.
can't find a parking place	You can't stop and rest. You can't find your "niche" in life.
car	Your vehicle on the "highway of life."
car keys	Your ability to open your mind to new things, to open yourself to the journey of life. It is the knowledge you don't think you know. When you lose your car keys, you are losing your ability to look within yourself and find your own answers. Keys are always the apparatus to give you answers. If you lose them, you are in a state of confusion.
car on fire	Possible fever or illness in the future. Or watch for a situation where you are "burned up" about something. Uncontrollable anger.
cell phone	Mobile mode of communication. In a car it brings the outside world right into your vehicle. If you dream of an accident in your car while you are talking on a cell phone, you are being warned to examine the influence or prevalence of the outer world in your life.

crossing a bridge	Going through a transition. A suspension bridge indicates that you may feel "suspended" and somewhat less than stable in your life.
danger ahead sign	Warning! Be careful.
dead battery	You're getting a warning that you may actually get a dead battery in your car. Or you are physically exhausted. Your daily energy is dissipating rapidly.
driver's license	Identification or permission to drive the car. You are overlooking an important detail in your everyday life. Losing your driver's license warns that you are losing control of your life or your identity.
driving backwards	Stepping back in your history
driving off a cliff	Watch out! Off the deep end. It may also be a new venture or beginning.
engine light on	You are coming unglued! Your brain is telling you that something is out of sync. It's time to look at things in your life to determine how to regain control.
flat tires	You're losing your grounding on a conscious level. It also indicates that you are exhausted. Time to rest up.
getting a new car	You need a change of perspective. It's time to update your goals or revitalize yourself. Consider finding a new means of expression.
getting the oil changed	Easy to interpret. This heads-up reminds you to have a tune-up for the car, or can it also be nudging you to get a physical check-up?

getting lost	You might need to look at details more carefully in some aspect of your life. Is there some scenario in your life where you feel "lost" or not in control?
highway	The highway of life. Look in the dream to see whether the road is smooth, straight, curvy or bumpy and apply the meaning.
hybrid car	This reflects your need to utilize and conserve your energy more consciously, more economically, and more efficiently. If you dream of driving a hybrid car, or if you actually purchase such a vehicle, then you are becoming more aware of using your energy more consciously, effectively, and efficiently. This may relate to your physical body energy, your money, or both.
license plate	Lets other people know you have a legal right to be on the road. You may need to look at what you are doing that may not be legal. Is the license plate clean and placed in the right place? Is it obscured, missing, or askew?
losing your car	Losing your self-esteem or feeling as if you have lost control of some aspect of your life.
lost keys	Carelessness or forgetting something in everyday life that will be important in the long run. Have you lost your ability to look within and find your own answers? Do you feel confused?
oil leak	This can be a literal indicator related to your car. Or you may have a circulatory problem in your body. There are too many fats in your system. This can also be a warning about your joints or a future cartilage problem.

out of gas	Body is tired. Go to bed and get rest. You have run out of energy.
police	Authorities. Check your dream to see if they are assisting you, restricting you, or reprimanding you. Watch for a situation in your life where an authority figure protects, warns, or disciplines you.
pushing your car	You are pushing yourself too hard. Moving forward, but in a way that exerts far too much energy.
rear-ended	You boundaries aren't clear. People are bumping into you. Get clear about your boundaries, especially related to the past. If you rear-end someone else, you are pushing their boundaries.
road signs	Messages. Apply the literal meaning of the signs. For example, if you see a yield sign in your dreams and it is significant in the dream, see if there is a situation in your life where you should yield to someone or something.
sideswiped	You are brushed by something or a situation nearby, but there is no danger.
smooth road	Things are going well or smoothly.
someone else is driving your car	Someone may be using your talents, ideas, energies, or abilities. Other may be taking advantage of you. The reverse is also true. If you are driving someone else's car, perhaps you are trying to exert control over that person's life or to take advantage of another person.
speeding ticket or warning	Moving too fast or breaking the rules. Your impulses are out of control.

spinning your wheels	You have lot of energy, but you aren't making any progress.
stolen car	Watch out for manipulation by others.
stopped by police	Police represent higher authority. Notice what the policeman did. Was there a penalty, reprimand, or just warning? Did he or she give you precautionary advice? What did you do in the dream?
stop sign	Stop. Is there a scenario in your life where you need to stop and take stock? Or just stop whatever you are doing?
stuck	If you dream that your car is stuck in traffic or mud, this may relate to a situation where you are unable to move forward. Try to identify who / what is blocking your forward progress. Or do you block your own progress by being a "stick in the mud?"
ticket	Disciplinary action involving some kind of payment on your part. It can relate to parking (being in a place that is not sanctioned or staying too long in one place.) Tickets also refer to pacing. Usually one is disciplined for going too fast, but it can happen for moving too slow.
traffic jam	Be patient; environmental conditions are slowing you down.
yield sign	Give in to whomever / whatever is going on.

5 color choices and your car

B elieve it or not, the color of the car you drive and the color of the upholstery inside will influence your driving behavior. The information below, based on Nancy Tappe's color theories, developed over years of research, will give you some guidelines about your own behavior behind the wheel and an explanation about the behavior of other drivers you observe on the road. But check it out for yourself. Enjoy yourself during your commute. As you sit in traffic, notice the cars around you. When you see erratic drivers on the road, notice the type and color of their vehicles. Watch for patterns and see for yourself: color matters.

color choice	Interpretation
black	Good choice for either car color or upholstery. Owners of black cars like to stay in control and like their own space. This color is neutral and will absorb agitation. It keeps the driver alert, awake, and focused on the drive. It keeps the car warmer in cold weather but absorbs heat in the summer. Black is one of the best all-around choices.

blue	Drivers of blue cars operate under a dual influence. They may look calm on the outside but be stressed on the inside. The blue color makes them feel calm, but it doesn't allow for rest. It quiets the stress rather than eliminating it. After a long trip in a blue car, passengers may be more tired than those who ride in cars with other colors. Blue is not an optimal color for the car – either in car color or in upholstery.
brown	A good color to own and drive. Brown cars are stable; they move well in traffic. They get where they are going safely. Brown upholstery keeps driver and passenger grounded.
burgundy	Good for long-term energy. Owners of burgundy cars are passionate active, earthy, and settled. They don't get tired of driving. They can drive forever.
gray	Gray is neutral and relaxing. It is calming and gives energy in a modified form. It is good for people who drive a lot. It is also a creative color. Drivers of gray cars are agile in traffic and able to shift easily from one lane to another in case of trouble. On a long trip, however, drivers of gray cars or cars with gray upholstery can get spacey and sleepy.

gold	Drivers of gold cars or cars with gold upholstery are often pushy and critical of others' driving. They will not lose control while driving, but when they get out of the car, they can be argumentative and lose control.
green	Green is the only color where shade or tint is important and the meaning changes from one to another.
avocado	Drivers of avocado cars will have a short patience level and can get agitated in traffic.
chartreuse	People who drive chartreuse cars are insecure behind the wheel.
forest green	Owners of forest green cars like to be in nature. They are outdoor people. They want to look successful. They are clear about what they want in their success, and they won't stop at anything to get it.
spring green	Drivers are natural and optimistic.
neon	Owners of neon cars are always dramatic. They want center stage and will take it, even on the road.

orange	People who drive orange cars can easily get spacey. They tend to forget to drive the car and let the car drive itself or drive as if no one else existed on the road.
pink	These car owners are emotional but efficient in stressful times. They can act quickly in emergencies on the road.
purple	They are highly dramatic. Everything is exaggerated. Drivers of purple cars also like center stage. They can also get explosive or angry if someone cuts in front of them or if things don't go their way.
red	Red is the most common universal color choice and the most visible. Drivers of red cars like to make sure everyone sees them and knows where they are. Owners are passionate; they have high energy levels and love activity. They don't necessarily accomplish more. They like to live their lives emotionally and physically. They are not always clear mentally. They do have a tendency to "push the pedal to the metal." It's a fun color to rent.
seafoam	This color is neutral and peaceful to drive. It is passive, and relaxed. Although rare, it is one of the better colors to own.

silver	A good color for calmness, but it can make the driver daydream and be spacey. People who drive metallic silver are dreamers who want quality, not quantity. They want only the best. They expect other drivers to be responsible.
tan	Drivers of tan cars like to take control. They are focused. They know what they want and pursue it completely. They are usually good drivers. Tan (in either leather or upholstery) is one of the best color choices. It calms and neutralizes the driver's agitation. A driver on tan upholstery is cool, collected, and careful. Leather breathes with you and is natural. It gives and stores energy. It calms the driver down in times of stress.
teal	Drivers of teal cars are impulsive. They like adventure and will race if you are interested.
two-tone	Owners of two-tone cars can be two personality types. White with any other color will alter that color and reduce it to a pastel in intensity. When two people have to drive the same car, two-tone is good.

white	White is the most common color for the average person. People who drive white cars stay in the middle of the road in their lives; they don't want to lead the pack. They are intimidated by the highway and they don't like accidents. White upholstery denotes elegance. It is an excellent choice for a neat person. It keeps the driver within himself. Drivers of cars with white upholstery are fastidious. They want quality in everything. A white car with tan upholstery is the safest of all choices.
yellow	This color indicates a car which shows detail easily. Police see this car first. Owners of yellow cars are highly intellectual and are impersonal to other people's feeling. Yellow is a good color for alertness. However, drivers of yellow cars think they own the freeway, and they like to speed.

What is the safest car to drive? White with tan upholstery. Other good choices include black, brown, burgundy, and seafoam.

6 frequently asked questions

Q: Whenever my car starts to break down, I just buy a new one. What kind of message is that?

A: Either your life is really moving along smoothly, or you are not willing to deal with messages that are there for you, should you choose to use them. You don't want to deal with things as they are.

Q: If a car reflects your life and current status, what does it mean when you buy a used car?

A: When you first buy a used car, it will initially retain the vibrations of the former owner. That can work well if it feels good to you, or it can feel uncomfortable. Eventually the former owner's vibrations will fade away, and the car will only reflect you.

Q: If I get my car fixed and pay the bill, does that naturally assume that the problem in my body is fixed?

A: Having your car repaired is your statement to the universe that you are ready to attract treatment or means of healing the ailment in your body. Or you are ready to deal with the life situation that needs revising. This can be done naturally or mechanically.

Q: What does it mean if you buy a new car, and it is a "lemon"?

A: You need to ask yourself why you picked this car. Analyze the parts that need repair. Ask yourself if you need to learn to live with it? Figure out what the message is for you. Or is there a situation in your life that you just need to learn to live with?

Q: I went to the glossary to find the interpretation for my car's malfunction, but I couldn't understand how that definition related to my life. What should I do?

A: Several things are possible. First, divide your car in half. The front of the car represents the future; the rear represents the past. The passenger area is, more or less, the present. If your auto's malfunction is in the future, perhaps you are getting a warning, and that accounts for not being able to link it to your body, mind, emotions, or life situations right now. But if it relates to the present or past, think through the general car system related to the malfunction. For example, if you needed to replace the master cylinder, and you can't see how that refers to you, then assess the fact that the master cylinder is part of the brake system. Is there part of your life where you need to take a break, give yourself a break, slow down, etc? Apply the over-all meaning of the system to your situation, and see if that helps. Then perhaps the specific part will take on more personal meaning.

Q: What does it mean if my daughter (or someone else) is driving my car and has an accident? Is the message for me or for her?

A: Apply the definitions from the glossary. Does it seem like the message is more appropriate for you or the other driver? Does it apply to you *and* your daughter together – in other words, you as a parent with her and the relationship that you have together?

Q: What is road rage? I see the most bizarre behavior on the road sometimes?

A: Unplanned drama. If you are a victim of road rage, ask yourself why you are willing to be victimized. Are you being victimized by someone you can't see? If you are the one in rage, examine your ability to control your anger.

Who / what is it that you are really angry at?

Q: I was on a business trip, and my rental car was stolen. What does that mean?

A: Having your car stolen in general relates to having something taken away from you that moves you from place to place. In other words your ability to think flexibility as you travel life's highway. With a rental car, it's a temporary situation. Look at where you were, what type of business you were transacting, and how that related to your thinking at the time.

Q: What does it mean if your car is broken into?

A: Some part of you is being abused or violated – physically, mentally, emotionally, or in a life situation. Look at the part of the car that was damaged. Use the glossary about that specific area of the car. This can also mean a virus or bacterial infection.

Q: I own several vehicles. How do I separate meanings from one car to another?

A: Look at how you use the vehicles. Is one strictly for work? Then car trouble with that vehicle would refer to situations with your work or job. Is one vehicle for leisure? Then you can interpret trouble there as it relates to vacations or recreation. But remember, your primary car relates to your daily life.

Q. What if I interpret the message wrong?

A: There are no "right" or "wrong" answers. Remember, you are the expert. Your car's message board emerges from *your* vibrations in *your* car. Use the general area of the car as a guideline, and the glossary. Even if you do not figure everything out, this process works in a cycle. The message will come around again.

Q: I don't own a car. I live in an urban area where I take the train to work. Occasionally I drive for recreation, but from day to day, I use public transportation.

A: Look for another machine in your life (other than a computer or television) that you use on a daily basis. See if you can work out some correlations. Your unconscious will always find a way to communicate with you if you are open.

Q: What does getting a new car mean?

A: It means a change of perspective or a new means of expression.

Q: What kind of messages are parking or speeding tickets?

A: Tickets represent disciplinary action involving some kind of payment or penalty on your part. They can relate to parking (being in a place that is not sanctioned or staying too long in one place.) Tickets also refer to pacing. Usually one is disciplined for going too fast, but it also can happen for moving too slowly.

Q: I recently broke off the key as I was trying to get into the car. I got some tweezers and was able to pull the broken part out of the lock. Fortunately I always carry a spare in my wallet. I got it out and immediately drove to a store where I got a replacement key made. What does all that mean?

A: First of all, it is wonderful that you did your own repair right there on the spot. Second, you carried a spare. So the implications of the message are minimal. To interpret this event, use the definition of keys and door locks. Keys represent your ability to open your mind to new things, to open yourself to the journey of life. You had the possibility of getting jammed or stuck in the driver side door lock. You were possibly jamming up your ability to be open to someone in your life who could give guidance or influence. But you were prepared for this, worked through it yourself, and went on your way.

7 car glossary

elow you will find an alphabetical listing of every car part and its corresponding relationship to your physical body, mind, emotions, or life situation. Then you will see questions you can ask yourself to determine what message your car is sending you. Remember that if you are the primary driver or if the car is yours, then the message is only for you.

Accelerator: increases or controls the forward movement and speed of the car. In relationship to the body or mind, it is an indicator of how you pace yourself. The accelerator in your car, therefore, mirrors your thyroid, the gland that balances or maintains balance in your metabolism, and the speed at which your metabolism works. If your thyroid is low, you don't have enough speed; if high, your energy is hyperactive. To take corrective action, you can ask yourself the following questions: Am I pacing myself correctly? Do I move too slowly or too fast? Do I rush through things in my life, or is there an area of my life where I feel too rushed? Do I need to adjust how I pace myself?

Air bags: safety devices on cars to protect driver and passengers during collision. As indicators of your safety and protection, they can relate to the skin or to weight you gain over a long period of time. They can also relate to flatulence. A malfunction with the airbag can be an indicator of your unconscious trying to tell you something that your conscious mind does not want to hear. Therefore, you might ask yourself to try to identify who or what you are not aware of. What am I afraid of? Who / what makes me feel unprotected or uncomfortable?

Air conditioning: controls temperature and humidity of the inside of the car. In your body this is represented by the thyroid or by your breathing. It can also indicate the endocrine system. Having your Freon replaced relates to updating your need to be regulated and comfortable for the future. The air conditioner can also be an early warning of problems with allergies. A malfunction here might lead you to ask yourself the following questions: Have I had dreams of suffocation or not being able to breathe properly? Is my breathing too shallow to support my health? Who / what is making me feel smothered? Do I need to quit smoking? Am I taking in some foods that I can't digest as well as I used to?

Air filter: traps and holds dirt to prevent flow into the carburetor or fuel injection system. In the body this relates to the nostrils, breathing, or liver difficulties. Difficulty here may also indicate food allergies. To pin down what this message means, you can ask yourself the following questions: What am I not tolerant of within myself? What in my life can I not tolerate? What skeletons (secrets) do I have that I consider dirty?

Alternator: (See also **Generator**) controls the use of electrical energy by producing alternating current (AC). In your body this relates to the central nervous system. To identify an alternator malfunction in your life, you might ask yourself the following questions: Do I need to be more mindful of releasing my stress? How do I release my stress? Have I been stressed so long that I don't recognize it anymore? Am I so stressed that it feels natural? Do I get headaches? Is my neck stiff? How can I begin releasing my tensions more systematically?

Alternator belt: flexible belt on front of engine that spins alternator to provide electricity to recharge battery. In the body this is represented by the adrenal glands. Replacing the alternator belt or having this particular belt break is an opportunity to ask some questions: Have I rested enough or too much? Have I released enough stress? Do I need to look at how I release my stress? Am I flexible in how I handle stress, or do I need to revise my stress management methods? Am I too rigid? Am I angry at myself for being less than I'd like to be?

Alternator light: warning indicator to check the alternator. It relates to your nervous system and to stress. If this light appears on the dashboard, you should identify the stressors in your life. You can ask yourself, is something stressing my heart? Am I right about what is going on in my life, or am I wrong? Am I doing well with my life or not doing that well? What will be the outcome of this? What will be the outcome if I don't make necessary changes? (Note: Sometimes this can be triggered by getting a ticket too.)

Antenna: sonar communication system bringing message from the outside world. This relates to your intuition. What do my feelings tell me? Am I listening to my inner wisdom? What are my options in this situation? If my antenna is broken off, how can I re-establish my intuition? Am I paying attention to my gut instincts?

Anti-lock brakes: braking system controlled by computer to reduce skids and prevent wheels from locking up on a slippery surface or when braking hard in an emergency. (Also see **brakes**) These are indicators of your thought processes. In a situation where these malfunction, you might ask yourself these questions: What do I need to concentrate on more? What am I doing that I need to think about more clearly? *What am I thinking?*

Axle: transfers power from differential to wheels. Feet and legs or circulation in the feet and legs represent this car part in the human body. The axle, then, relates to energy as it moves through the lower part of the body. Messages in your car in the axle require you to ask yourself: What aspect of my life isn't moving smoothly? Do I need to exercise my legs more? Should I get to the gym or add a daily walk regimen? What aspect of my life do I need to create new movement in?

Back seat: area for passengers behind the driver. It relates to the here and now with a slight past orientation. The right side is your outer world. The left side of the back seat is your inner world. You can ask yourself, who is pressuring me to do what I am not doing? Something wrong with the back seat may indicate that something is wrong with your present or recent past. Have you taken a back seat in a situation that feels uncomfortable? Is it time for you to take control? Or vice versa?

Back-up lights: indicate that the car is moving backward. This function on the car indicates how you communicate your past history to others. A malfunction here can indicate mental vacillation about past events and not turning loose of things or not communicating to others what you have turned loose of. Replacing a back-up light may mean that you are clearer about communicating your past to others. If you have a broken light, you might want to ask yourself: What do I need to let go of from the past? Am I communicating my past clearly to others?

Battery: source of energy for the car which generates and stores electrical energy and stabilizes voltage in the electrical system. The battery is the most important message center in your car. It symbolizes your metabolism and awareness and indicates how energy moves through your body. It can also relate to your reproductive system or your electrolytes. When you get low in energy to the point that the adrenals are not producing electrolytes, you need to rest, but not to the point that you begin to atrophy. The battery symbolizes your "charge" on life. A dead battery warns that you are exhausted physically, mentally, or emotionally. Therefore, when the battery is dead, it is time to ask yourself: What do I need to do to recharge myself? Is it food, exercise, meditation, a vacation, a new hobby? Buying a new battery or battery cables requires you to ask yourself: What do I need to release in order for me to not feel drained? What is draining me? How can I conserve my energy? Do I need to prioritize? Am I trying to be superman or superwoman? What or who balances and/or energizes me? Do I have some kind of activity where I can renew myself daily? The **battery cable** is your vision of what you want to create. If it is rusty, corroded, or needs replacing, then ask yourself what you need to clean up or replace in your view of what you want to create in your life.

Bearings: reduce the amount of friction between fixed and moving parts of the car. They relate to your equilibrium and flexibility. The bearings also relate to the tendons between your joints. Problems here could indicate the start of arthritis or stiffening of your joints. A malfunction here could also indicate balance problems. It's time to ask yourself: How can I be more flexible? What areas of my life require more flexibility on my part? What or who is rubbing me the wrong way or causing friction in my life? Am I being stubborn and unchangeable? Do I need a new attitude? What or who causes me to stiffen up or to be less flexible?

Belts: flexible, endless bands around wheels or pulleys to assure smooth, continuous motion. They represent the ligaments and tendons in the body. A broken belt or replacing a belt gives you the opportunity to ask yourself: Am I stretching my joints enough but not too much? Am I flexible in my attitude in the world? Do I get angry in my body when I can't stretch the way I want to? Is this a good time for a yoga class? If a belt breaks, you can ask yourself if you have become too rigid, too inflexible, or too angry at yourself for being less than you'd like to be.

Blinker: directional signals (left, right, and hazard) to others. The blinker indicates your attitude and how you communicate your intentions to others. People who have trouble here are those who don't communicate their feelings or intentions to other people. Hazard lights indicate to others to keep their distance. They signal that you aren't objective any more. You are so wrapped up in yourselves and your "stuff" that you can't see clearly. So it's time to question: In what area of my life am I having trouble communicating my feelings or intentions? How clear am I to others? Am I only thinking of myself?

Body: metal shell encompassing interior car parts and the passenger area. Pings, dings, or scratches here relate to your skin. Body rust can warn of skin problems or skin cancer, or it can be a reaction to outer elements. When the surface of the body of your car is marred in some way, then it's a good idea to ask yourself: Do I have sensitive skin? How do I handle the world? Am I thin-skinned or thick-skinned? Am I literally having trouble with my skin? Should I see a dermatologist? Or does this malfunction correspond to how I relate to the world. Are my boundaries clear? Do they work?

Brakes: slow down or stop your car: Brakes refer to an entire system within the car and consist of many parts. Brakes refer to your feet or your immune system. They also relate to your sense of discipline, self-control, and your will-power. Trouble here is a warning that you that might need to stop and take a break. You may have lost control over your life. You have lost your ability to stop the forward motion of events. You are over-working and should slow down. Problems here might also mean stiff toes or poor circulation in the feet such as spurs, calluses,

Achilles heel problems, blisters, pulled tendons, etc. In terms of your ability to slow down, a malfunction in the braking system could relate to eating or drinking something (usually a high-calorie sugar substance) to keep going. Having to replace the brakes gives you the opportunity to ask yourself: Am I pushing my body too far? Do I need to slow down? How can I nurture myself more? How can I figure out when to keep going and when to stop? Do I have a sense of how much is too much? Do I need a break? Can I allow myself to stop and re-evaluate my pace? Am I getting the wrong kind of booster? Do I live on false energy, i.e. caffeine, energy drinks, or overeating? Can I carry an average pace, or am I too slow or too fast? Do I exercise enough to keep the flow through my body? Am I limber? Do I stop when I need to for rest and revitalization? Do I wear the right type shoes? How well do I protect myself? Am I grounded? Do I feel like I have no control over my life? Am I unable to stop the forward motion of events in my life?

Bumper: protective device on front and rear of your car. The bumper used to be protective; now it's primarily cosmetic. It relates to the energy field around you. It reflects your energy and how you use it, as well as how the world perceives your energy. The bumper will not help you in a time of crisis. Problems with the bumper allow you to ask yourself: What options can I use to change and improve what I'm doing? What can I do to develop a protective edge to my life? How can I become aware of the differences between my energy and my body? Are my boundaries superficial? Am I aware of my boundaries? Am I vulnerable?

Carburetor: mixes fuel and air and delivers them to the combustion chamber to produce energy. (See **Fuel Injection System**) The carburetor refers to your liver or heart. Trouble here gives you the opportunity to ask yourself: Am I breathing properly? Am I aware that if I'm not breathing properly, then my liver cannot purify toxins properly and give me more energy? Do I need to take some steps to detoxify my body? Do I need some exercise or yoga to improve the quality of my breathing? Am I getting the right vitamins and minerals in my body? Does the food I eat provide proper energy for all my activities?

Cargo rack: area on top of car for transporting goods. The cargo rack symbolizes the arms and back. They relate to part of the ego. If something falls off, then it is time to ask: What am I carrying that is heavier than I can handle? Am I carrying something that really isn't mine to carry? If the cargo rack breaks off, what is it in my life that I can no longer carry? Or can I continue to handle such heavy loads? Do I carry around too much "stuff?"

Car keys: metal instruments to gain or restrict entrance. Car keys represent your ability to unlock the mysteries of life. They are always the apparatus to give answers. They show you your ability to open yourself to life's journey. They are the knowledge you don't think you know. When you lose your car keys, you are losing your ability to look within yourself and find your answers. You are confused. It's time to ask yourself: What is confusing me? What do I think I know, but I may refuse to acknowledge? What new ideas am I closed off to? What am I ignoring? **Trunk key:** the key to unlock the place you store your past or your memories.

Cassettes, CD player, radio, IPod: devices to bring music, news, or information into the car. They are your ears—hearing the outside world for pleasure and learning. These devices represent your modern communication from the outside world and what you allow in from the outside world. If one of these devices breaks, you have lost your connection to the following areas: If it's motivational tapes or information, you are overloaded, and none of it is digesting properly. If it's music, you are blocked in your recreation, entertainment, amusement, or stress management. Difficulties here call for you to question yourself in the following areas: Am I listening carefully to the world around me? Are people, places, and events trying to tell me things that I'm just not hearing? Am I blocking information? Am I chattering in the outer world in order to keep from hearing my inner voice? Am I so busy listening to the chatter of the outer world that I don't hear my inner voice?

Cell phone / car phone: portable telephone enabling communication from inside the car. Your cell phone is your communication to the outside world via a receptor. An accident that occurs while you are on the cell phone is a serious warning to you about your relationship with the outer world and its prevalence in your life. Am I hearing and communicating clearly with the outside world? Is the outside world so dominant in my life that I can't be in charge and put it aside while I'm driving?

Chassis: the under frame on which the body of the car is mounted and to which the engine with all the drive train components are secured. The chassis refers to your skeleton. Trouble with the chassis warns you to ask yourself: Am I structurally healthy? Am I having bone trouble?

Choke: controls ratio of fuel to air in carburetor when the engine is cold. The choke is an indicator in the body of your circulation and blood system and their effect on your heart. Trouble here gives you an opportunity to ask yourself: What pumps me up and gets me going? Do I need a jumpstart? You can also examine the literal implications: do I choke sometimes? What causes it? Is it time to get this checked out?

Clock: device to indicate time. Trouble here indicates that you are out of touch with your age and that there is a conflict with your timing. If your clock stops, you can ask yourself the following questions: Am I in correct timing? Is my timing in life off? Do I feel like I am keeping pace with time? Am I in sync with what's going on around me? Am I able to keep up? Adjusting your clock in the spring or fall with the seasonal time change allows you to rethink these issues in your life.

Clutch: part of the transmission that helps transfer power from the engine and assists in shifting gears. It helps get the car in gear. (See also **Torque Converter)** The clutch refers to your adrenals, and it is the part that gets you going. It is your motivation and, more important, your ability to act on your motivation. It is also your ability to balance your nerves. When a problem appears here, it's time to question: What stops me? How can I motivate myself and follow through with my desires and goals? What kind of incentive do I need to finish things through to completion? Am I too intense inside?

Coil: conducts electricity from the battery to the distributor. It symbolizes your heart valves. Trouble warns that you are getting sluggish and not taking care of yourself. You need to watch your diet and exercise moderately to stimulate the circulation. Now you can ask yourself: What am I lackadaisical about? What can I do to get charged back up again? What is zapping my motivation? How can I re-energize myself?

Combustion chamber: area in cylinder where air and fuel mixture ignites. This refers to the adrenals in the body. If there is trouble here, you are too exhausted. You must give yourself time to rest and restore your energy. The warning might suggest that you ask some questions: How can I slow down and rest? In what area of my life am I pushing too hard? How can I learn to say "no"?

Compressor: part of the air conditioning system that moves the coolant through the air conditioning system. It is the body's triple warmer. It relates to the hormones, thyroid, and adrenal system. Questions to ask are: Am I balanced? Are my hormones balanced? Where am I out of balance? How can I balance myself? Do I get carried away with my passion, or do I not allow myself time for my passion? Is there a proper working balance between my body and mind?

Condenser: part of air conditioning system that changes refrigerant from a gas to a liquid. The condenser refers to your circulation, liver, or kidneys. It may indicate that your circulation is off its best pace for yourself. You need to pace yourself, depending on what is normal for your individual body. You can ask yourself: What do I need to let go of or release in my mind or in my life? Am I always in a hurry? Or am I going through life at a snail's pace, and I need to get moving?

Coolant: mixture of water and chemicals that move through engine to maintain the proper temperature. This relates to your blood pressure and nervous system. This auto part refers to how you keep calm and cool. Trouble here indicates that you aren't stabilized in your emotions. You might want to ask yourself: What can I do to create more stability in my life? What do I need to do to become more stabilized? What do I have an emotional charge on that causes me to feel out of control?

Crank case: provides a reservoir for lubrication of oil and houses the oil pumps. In the body this corresponds to the blood vessels and heart. Trouble here indicates that you need to clean up your diet, food and drink intake. You need to exercise or get a health program. You can ask yourself: What do I need to do to modify my diet or start a new health regime? Am I drinking too much alcohol? Am I eating too much junk food?

Cruise control mechanism: drives the car automatically in forward motion. This relates to your self-discipline and self-pacing. Problems indicate that you can't stay correctly on course. You need self-discipline. You might ask yourself: How have I lost control of myself or my response to the events around me? How can I get back on course at a regulated pace? How do I need to adjust my pacing so that I "cruise along" automatically?

CV joint (constant velocity joint): allows drive axle to move at a constant speed when a front-wheel drive car turns. In body terms, this is your equilibrium. It relates to your reactions to people and places around you. It is a good time to ask these questions: What or who is causing me to lose my sense of balance? What can I do to restore my emotional equilibrium?

Cylinder: (see **Master cylinder** or **engine cylinder**)

Dashboard: houses the controls for the car and gives messages to the driver about what's going on within the auto. In the body these parts are the brain and skull. They are your heads-up or alert system. Normal messages from the dashboard indicate that your internal message system works well, and there is no problem. However, when a warning light appears on the dashboard, you need to ask yourself the following questions: What does my conscious mind keep telling me that I'm not listening to? What am I avoiding or denying? What do I not want to hear? Or what do I want to hear so much that I don't hear what is actually being said? Am I filtering information so that I only hear what I want?

Differential: an assembly of gears which transfers power from transmission to rear axles and then to rear wheels. This is now a high-tech area with many parts. It relates to your circulation. You may need to watch for breathing or elimination problems. It is time to get moving. You can't just have the upper part of the body working without the lower part working too and vice versa. Ask yourself: How harmonious am I in my everyday living with people, places, and events around me? Am I stuck in my actions, my thinking, or my feelings? Or is my head telling me one thing, but I just can't seem to put it into action?

Dipstick: measures amount of liquid in chamber for oil, brakes, and transmission. In your auto it signifies your hunger or thirst. The dipstick is the body's measuring device to determine what you need to do to keep yourself happy and comfortable. Every time you check oil, automatic transmission fluid, or brake fluid, you need to ask yourself if you need anything to fill yourself up emotionally. If the dipstick breaks, it could indicate an eating disorder. It's time to ask yourself the following questions: Am I satisfied and productive in my life? Am I content with who I am and where I am? What am I hungering for that I am not aware of? Do I thirst for some bit of knowledge that I do not have current information about? Am I overworking?

Distributor: part of the ignition system that applies electrical current in proper sequence to the spark plugs. It is your circulation. Questions to ask include: Is my energy being distributed well throughout my body? Do I exercise enough to keep my circulation functioning smoothly?

Door handle: allows opening and closing of doors. It is your solar plexus. A problem with your door handles invites you to ask yourself the following questions: Am I bringing the right things into my body, or am I releasing the right things? Am I open to the right things coming from the world? Am I sending the right things out into the world?

Doors: exits and entrances to your auto. They refer to your elimination system (exits), and your bodily orifices for air and food intake (entrances). Doors represent your opportunities or openings to your inner self and your outer world. The left front door signifies what you are doing today to create tomorrow. The left rear door refers to what you are doing today to access the past. The right front door relates to what you are doing today in the outer world for tomorrow. The right rear door signifies what you are doing today in the outer world to access your past. You might ask yourself the following questions: Am I open or closed to the past and the future at the right times and for the right reasons? Am I as careful with the things I put into my body or that I repel from my body? Am I open or closed to new opportunities in my life? Am I aware of how I deal with my past?

Door locks: security devices around the elimination system as well as other security devices for the body. They may relate to the skin or to your mental process as a security system. Automatic locks signify a point in your evolution when you are automatically protected. You can ask: Where don't I feel protected or secure? Am I cautious about being out in the world alone? Am I always aware of my security? If the door is locked and will not unlock, am I closed to allowing someone in my life to give guidance or influence? If door lock is easy to penetrate by others, you might not feel safe about who comes into and out of your life from the outside world.

Drive axle: (See **four-wheel drive** and **rear-wheel drive)** connects the transaxle to the front wheels. The drive axle signifies your feet (the portable part that moves the entire body) and parts of the brain. It relates to how well you follow or how well you coordinate leading and following. You can ask: If I don't see where I'm going, how will I know where to put my feet? Am I on solid footing? Am I clear about my direction? Do I have my feet on the ground?

Drive shaft: (See **rear-wheel drive**) connects the transmission to the differential in rear-wheel-drive cars. It refers to your muscles. People who drive rear-wheel cars lead by following, i.e. they use other people's advice. Front-wheel drivers lead on their own initiative. Questions to ask with problems in the drive shaft are: How good or valid is the advice I follow? Have I lost my passion / initiative? Am I having problems as a leader or follower?

ECU (electronic control unit): a small computerized system which analyzes information and adjusts the operation of the fuel and emission systems. A malfunction will cause the "Check Engine" light to come on. In the body this is the brain, warning you that something is out of sync. You need to check where you are; you're coming unglued. It's time to ask: How do I get back in control or balance? If I'm shifting out of control, what control of myself have I lost? How do I regain my power? What created the situation that has me out of control? How do I resolve it for me?

Electrical wiring system: provides electrical current to start and operate all the electrical parts of the car. This is your nervous system. You need more balance in your life. You can ask yourself some questions: How sensitive am I to change? How easily do I balance change in my life? Do I go with the flow or fight change? Am I trying to do too many things at once? What do I need to do to balance things out?

Electronic ignition: what gets the car started, different from the old "points" system. It is your motivation, your muscles, brain, nervous system, and vision. Trouble here might motivate you to ask yourself: Am I in harmony with myself? Do I see things clearly? Do I want to do the things I have to do? Do I do a lot of brain chatter?

Electronic power steering (EPS): a computerized steering system that controls and improves steering control by increasing the pressure applied to the steering linkage, thus reducing driver effort to manually turn the steering wheel. In the body this refers to your brain and circulation. A malfunction in the EPS indicates that you should ask yourself the following questions: Do I have enough energy going to my brain to keep me alert? Am I in control mentally? Do I feel out of it? Connected? Am I spacing out? Am I aware of what is happening around me? Do I daydream too much?

Emission system: (See **smog check**) keeps air clear and controls substances that allow exhaust. This system refers to the lungs, liver, and lymphatic system. You need to clean up your act. You have too many preservatives or pollutants in your body. With this problem you can ask yourself: What can I do for a complete body cleansing, internally as well as externally? Who, what, or where in my life is toxic to my system? How do I take better care of my health? What do I need to do to restore health and balance to my body? Is it time to clean out my system from all the fast foods or processed foods?

Engine: what makes the car run. It is your heart, your chest, your motivation, or your ability to keep going. An engine tune-up indicates a need for a physical check-up. It's time to rest and recharge the whole system. It's time to balance your entire living condition. You can consider the following questions: Am I a workaholic? Am I too busy being social to focus on work? Or have I lost all my drive and motivation? What adjustments/ refinements can I make with my life to get things flowing more smoothly again? If the check engine light comes on, you are coming unglued! Your brain is telling you that something is out of sync. It's time to look at things in your life to determine how to regain control.

Engine cylinder: a hollow area in engine where piston is found. In the body it relates to your aorta. Trouble here asks you to question: Am I open to new information? Am I flexible in my view of things? Am I aware that the car is talking to me? Am I willing to change things that are not satisfactory to me, or do I become a victim?

Exhaust: what the car eliminates. The exhaust is your colon, your elimination system, or your kidneys. A choice factor. You can ask yourself: What am I holding on to that I should let go of? Do I eliminate toxins from my body easily or with difficulty? Do I have the possibility of eliminating things from my life that aren't satisfactory?

Evaporator core: part of air conditioning system that changes refrigerant from a liquid to a gas and absorbs heat from air. This relates to the endocrine system. Problems arising here call for the following question: What do I need to do to regulate my life? What do I need to adjust to lead a more healthy life?

Exhaust manifold: leads exhaust gases from engine to exhaust system. It refers to the small intestine. You can ask yourself: How do I evaluate my present experiences and separate them from the past and the future? What am I willing to release from the past or not create in the future?

Fan: keeps the engine cool. In the body this refers to your circulation, your lungs or bronchial area, or to your thyroid or thymus. Problems in the fan ask you to pose some questions: How well am I taking care of my body to keep it in balance? Am I honest with myself? Do I tell the world one thing and feel something else? Do I have an inner / outer conflict?

Fan belt: connects spinning motor to fan on front of motor which draws cool outside air into engine bay to cool motor. It fits around the generator. In the body, the fan belt corresponds to the valves to heart. Some difficulty here might require you to ask yourself: How do I maintain emotional balance? Am I emotionally out of balance? What can I do to regain that balance?

Fenders: guard the wheels of the car. Front fenders refer to your shoulders and balance system. They deal with your ideals, goals, and dreams. Back fenders refer to your hips and deal with your reality. Fenders can also relate to the outer part of the body, how you look in the world. You can quiz yourself: Are my dreams unrealistic? Do I need a different dream? Do I need to take baby steps to reach that bigger goal? Am I stuck in what I am doing? Do my feelings get hurt easily? Do I have poor self-esteem? Fender benders indicate a block in these areas.

Filters: keep the car clean. They can refer to your liver and lungs. A problem in this area calls for you to ask yourself: What can I do to clean up my act? Do

I periodically rest and cleanse my body? Replacing a filter provides a good time to do a quick detox and get some extra rest.

Firewall: barrier between engine compartment and passenger compartment. It is your immune system, and a problem with your firewall asks you to consider the following: Do I have clear boundaries? Do I need to re-evaluate or reset my boundaries?

Fluids: (oil, transmission, brake, windshield washer, power steering) liquids used to lubricate various parts of the car. Fluids literally relate to the fluids within your body: tear ducts, urinary tract: kidneys, bladder, etc. They refer to your cleansing process. Each time you add fluid to the car, you should cleanse your body too. This is a good time to ask: How clear am I? Am I taking care of myself inside my body and in my mind? Am I honest with myself? Do I use honest precautions with things that could lead to illness? Do I keep my mind and body balanced?

Four-wheel drive: (See **drive shaft**): a vehicle equipped with both front and rear differential to transmit power to all four wheels. Four-wheel drive refers your muscles. A malfunction might ask you to consider the following: Is my body geared to rough and ready pursuits, or is it more streamlined to aesthetic processes? Do I have freedom to move where or when I want? Do I move smoothly, or am I stiff? Am I well-coordinated, or is my coordination off?

Front-wheel drive: (See transaxle) this car part relates to the muscles. Front-wheel drivers lead on their own initiative. Problems require you to ask yourself: Am I an initiator? Am I a self-starter? Do I accomplish what I set out to?

Fuel: food for the car which provides energy for the car to operate. This correlates to food, water, or air, and your breathing, eating, or drinking. So you can ask yourself: What am I taking in? What do I feed myself? Do I eat the right food, drink enough fluids, and breathe properly? Am I getting enough nutrients for my body to function well?

Fuel injection system: makes sure exact amount of pressurized fuel is released into each combustion chamber. It replaces the old **carburetor.** This system corresponds to your breath. It determines how you are eating your food and how food moves throughout your body. Difficulties here require you to ask yourself: Am I really enjoying the food I eat? Does what I eat seem to be working for my body? What changes could I make? Is it time to evaluate my diet?

Fuel pump: pressurizes the fuel system to move gas from tank to engine. In the body this correlates to the spleen or the large intestine. Trouble here indicates that you are taking in food that you aren't assimilating. You can ask yourself: Does my energy move freely through my system, or am I able to process everything I take in? Having to replace a fuel pump is a message to you that it's time to re-evaluate and make changes with your diet. Having to buy a new fuel pump says it's time for a new diet.

Fuses: small electrical devices which cut current in overloaded circuits. They refer to your electrolytes and to your adrenals. A problem with the fuses or the necessity to replace a fuse requires you to ask yourself the following: Do I keep my body balanced in energy? Am I ready to "blow a fuse" about something? How can I regain balance with this challenge?

Gas: fuel for car. Putting gas in the tank correlates to the food you put into your body. When you buy gasoline, it's time to mentally question yourself: Am I doing the right thing for me? Am I getting what I need to function properly? Does what I eat or drink keep my body functioning smoothly? Is my breathing tight and restrictive?

Gas cap: cap on spout to gas tank prevents foreign materials from entering fuel. It relates to your sinuses. You can ask yourself: Am I using the air I take in properly? Am I careful about what I put into my body, or do I allow poor food choices or poor breathing to enter my body?

Gasket: sealers or soft materials used to seal areas between non-moving parts. The gasket relates to how you keep your emotions under control. You can ask yourself: How real can I be with myself to handle or not handle what's going on in my life? Are there any situations in my life where I "blow my gasket" with people, places, or events? What do I need to do to get this under control?

Gas tank: holds the fuel. In the body the gas tank corresponds to the stomach or to the digestive tract. Running out of gas indicates that you have run out of energy or enthusiasm. It's time to rest, recharge and "feed" yourself. If you run out of gas, it's time to ask yourself: How am I handling the information coming to me from the outside world? Am I digesting it well? How well do I tolerate my intake? Am I eating properly? Drinking adequately?

Gear shift: apparatus used to change gears. It can refer to your flexibility or how you shift gears from one aspect of your life to another. Problems with the gear shift require you to question: Am I flexible? Can I move from one thing to another without breaking down? How easily do I accept periods of transition or moving from one thing to another?

Generator: (See **alternator**) produces direct current (DC). Fan belt fits around the outside. The generator correlates to the central nervous system. With generator problems, you need to ask yourself: How smoothly do I accept change? Is change easy for me? Is it difficult? How well am I tolerating the changes in my life?

GPS system: vision, ability to go where you want to go. This system relates to your motivation, your overview of life, and your ability to move yourself through life according to the way you plan. A faulty system requires you to ask yourself: Am I aware of where I am and what I am doing? Am I self-motivated? Do I accomplish my goals?

Grill: decorative metal at front of car. It corresponds to your nose. The grill is a cosmetic function. In the car it always deals with self-esteem. Dents or accidents in the grill indicate that you might want to ask yourself: How do I accept myself? Do I like me? How do I feel about who I am?

Hatchback: opening to cargo area. It is a cosmetic function, and it correlates to your past. How comfortable am I with my past? Have I integrated it to my satisfaction?

Hazard lights: (See **blinker**)

Head gasket: helps contain pressure in the cylinders. It seals off pressure between the cylinder and the engine block. The head gasket refers to your circulation system or to the lymphatic system. Blowing a head gasket is definitely the time to ask: How well do I accept change and stress in the world? Am I stubborn about change? Do I blow up about things?

Headlights: attached to front end of car to illuminate the road ahead. Headlights are your eyes or your vision. Replacing a headlight is a good time to ask: Am I seeing things as they are? Am I being idealistic or pessimistic about what I see in the world? Am I clearly seeing what's going on around me?

Heater: keeps car warm on inside. It refers to your hormone system. A faulty or non-functioning heater invites you to investigate the following questions: Do I feel normal and accepted in the world? Am I staying regulated? Am I burning the food that I am putting in my body adequately to run my system correctly? Am I exercising enough?

Hood: moveable part of the body of car that covers the engine. It is the part of the car that protects the engine and inner workings of the auto. It protects and covers. The message here is to calm down. Things are not as bad as they look. Be patient. Damage to the hood is a shock point. Ask yourself, has anything come to a big surprise to me lately? Is a shock coming?

Horn: electrical device which makes noise to warn pedestrians or other motorists. Your car horn is your voice or your vocal chords. It is your warning system. It indicates how you warn others. Horn problems require you to ask the following questions: Do I communicate clearly? Do I know how to get people's attention when I need help? When the horn is stuck, am I shouting and no one is listening? Do I speak up for myself? If horn doesn't sound, am I communicating in a way that others can hear me? Do I rest my vocal chords enough not to abuse them?

Hoses: flexible rubberized tubes used to convey fluids. They refer to your tendons or to your valves. Replacing a hose is a good time to ask yourself: How well do I communicate in the world? How capable am I of holding things together? Am I connected to the big picture? If a hose breaks, I can ask myself about what aspect of my life is disconnected or broken. What am I currently really upset about? Where have I lost flexibility?

Hub caps: dressing to the tire. If you lose a hub cap, you are one who is not grounded or who is in denial about being grounded. You might ask yourself: Am I grounded? What can I do to become more grounded or more stable in my life?

Idle: condition of engine when running without any application of the accelerator. The idle is the same as the lungs or the breath in your body. If your car vibrates in idle, you are going too fast or too slow. You get nervous when you stand still. You don't know how to be "idle." You should ask yourself: Do I breathe properly? When I'm stressed, do I hold my breath?

Ignition system: fires the engine. This corresponds to your adrenals or to your motivation, and it indicates how you get started. It is your ability to be a self-starter. Difficulties in the ignition system should motivate you to ask yourself: Am I self-motivated, or do I depend on someone else to get me started? Do I lean on other people, or do I make my own moves? What gets me going? What makes me passionate about life?

Intake manifold: allows fuel and air mixture to enter the cylinders from the carburetor in an evenly distributed manner. The manifold relates to the heart valves or to the bronchial area. Trouble in this area invites you to question: Am I able to talk and think at the same time? Am I able to think and act at the same time? Have I got it together? Do other people see me as someone who has it together?

Intake valve: allows fuel and air mixture to enter the combustion chamber. This relates to the lungs, the nasal passages, or to the mouth. A malfunction in the intake valve asks you to ask yourself: Am I breathing properly? Do I keep my nasal passages and mouth clear and clean?

License plate: designates the car's official identity. It is your identification system to the outside world or your face. Replacing the license plate or a defective plate calls for you to question: Does the world see who I am? What message do I want to send the world? Am I clear about how I define myself to others?

Lights: indicates your intentions to others. See **blinker.**

Lubrication: prevents friction between parts as they run the car. It reduces wear and tear on parts of the car. The lubrication represents the cartilage between joints or the tendons. You can ask yourself: Am I staying flexible in the world, or am I getting stiff and rigid?

Main bearings: cushion the contact of the spinning crankshaft with the engine block. They refer to your brain. Malfunctioning bearings require you to ask: Is my brain functioning for clear thinking? Does my brain get clouded during stress moments? How quickly am I able to clear my thinking?

Manifold: facilitates the intake or exhaust of air to or from the engine. The manifold corresponds to your lungs. Repairing or replacing the manifold is a good time to check yourself: Do I have problems that I've ignored purposefully that I need to deal with? Are my lungs healthy? If I am a smoker, is this a sign that I need to quit? Am I in a toxic environment where the air is unclean and damaging to my respiratory system?

Master cylinder: (See **brake**) stores brake fluid, produces pressure in the brake system, and assists or magnifies one's ability to slow the car without effort. It is the energy run by your adrenals. A problem here invites you to ask yourself: What is preventing me from knowing when and where to stop what I'm doing for the good of my body? Where is this knowledge blocked?

Mirrors: a reflective device which allows drivers a view of the side or rear of vehicle. They are your hindsight or your reflective vision. The rearview and side mirrors look to the past to see what's coming up. The right-hand mirror is always distorted in distance (in the United States); the left is always clear. Repairing or replacing the mirrors ask you to question: How often do I do things that are not appropriate in timing? Am I out of sync? Is my behavior inappropriate at times? Do I speak before I think? Am I able to gauge things in the right hand mirror (my view of the outer world) correctly even though it is distorted?

Muffler: softens or reduces noise made by engine. The muffler corresponds to the lining in ears or filters in nose. It also represents your bronchial area. Trouble indicates that you are not staying stabilized within your own energy level. Muffler difficulties ask you to contemplate: Am I unable to stabilize my energy level? Trouble indicates that my energy is not stabilized. What do I need to do to balance and stabilize my energy?

Oil: primary lubricant. It relates to your blood and other lubricants in your system, which keeps your joints from stiffening. Replacing the oil is a good time for you to ask yourself: Am I flexible and mobile enough? Do I go with the flow?

Oil filter: protects the quality of engine oil by trapping and holding contaminants. The filter correlates to your liver or to your lymphatic system. Buying a new filter is a good time for you to ask yourself: Do I clean my system regularly to keep it balanced and clear?

Oil pump: brings oil to engine. The pump refers to your circulation or your responses to people, places, and events in the world. Problems here indicate that your actions and reactions are not normal? Am I over-reacting to people or situations in my life?

Oxygen sensor: measures amount of oxygen in the exhaust and monitors amount of air or fuel ratio being burned. This sensor refers to your esophagus or your diaphragm. Having a problem with this sensor is a good time to ask yourself: Why am I holding back from what is available to me from life? What fears are stopping me? Do I feel guilty if I am successful?

Pedal: activates and controls forward or stopping capability. It is your thinking about going forward or about stopping. Replacing the pedal or a stuck pedal allows you the opportunity to evaluate the following: Am I in charge of or in control of going forward with my life or of stopping something I am doing?

PCV filter: keeps inside of engine clean and reduces air pollution. It is your liver. Difficulties in this area give you the opportunity to think through the following: How well do I distinguish between good energy coming to me vs. bad energy? Do I have set boundaries? Am I aware of what they are? Do I have clarity about issues or problems as they present themselves to me? Do I literally need a liver cleanse, or it time to clean up my act regarding my energy?

Pistons: compresses air / fuel mixture to be ignited for power. Pistons are your digestive tract or your ability to assimilate nutrients and caloric processes within food. Problems here indicate that you should ask yourself: Can I easily bring about what I want? Am I productive? Am I distracted easily? Do I recognize my blocks? Do I have trouble assimilating new information or situations?

Radiator: circulates air through the coolant to keep engine cool. The radiator refers to your glandular system, your heart, and kidneys. It is your awareness and your perception. It also relates to whatever raises or lowers your temperature. Repairing or replacing your radiator calls for you to ask yourself: How balanced am I? Am I keeping all parts working together so I am balanced and healthy? If your radiator overheats, ask yourself, am I hot under the collar? What is making me angry? Do I have a fever?

Radio: device for receiving wireless transmissions from outside world. It is your ears or your communication with the outside world to you. A defective radio means you should ask yourself: Am I hearing correctly? Is what I think I hear what the other person is actually communicating? Am I capable of making that evaluation? Am I wise enough to know the difference?

Rear-wheel drive: (See **drive shaft)** this car part relates to your muscles. Trouble with this drive suggests that you ask yourself: Am I capable of following instructions, even though I might think I know a better way? Can I be a follower when necessary?

Roof: top protective covering of the car. It corresponds to your hair or scalp and relates to your strength. Ask yourself, am I being as strong as I can be, or am I playing the victim?

Seat belt: straps passengers to seats for security purposes in case of fast braking or collision. It is your safety factor, a self-imposed limitation and safeguard. You can ask yourself: Am I secure enough to feel safe? Can I evaluate my safety? Do I know where my boundaries are? Do I feel safe at night in my world? Am I safe at work? Am I aware of the safe bounds of my energy level, and do I respect them? Do I burn out easily? Am I feeling too strapped down?

Security system: automatic device to take measures to prevent theft of car or belongings of occupants. This system is the same as your ego. Issues involving your security system can be resolved by asking yourself: Do I listen to warnings my body gives me? Do I know the difference between what my body knows and what my head says? Do I know the difference between what my head knows and what the world is saying? Do I listen to my intuition? Can I trust my own judgment?

Sensors: monitor engine condition and functions and feed this data to car's computer (Electronic Control Module). The sensors echo your intuition or your sense of what is about to happen. You can ask yourself these questions: Am I aware enough to sense my safety or danger around me? Do I know my boundaries with other people, places, and events? Do I sense danger around me?

Shock absorbers: air pressure devices found near each wheel to smooth out the up and down motion of the car; they keep passengers from losing control when the car hits a bump or hole. Shocks keep car level during braking. They represent the discs between joints, your spinal discs. When a question arises in this area of the car, you should ask yourself: Am I aware when I am putting stress on my joints? Do I overwork my joints and feel pain after the fact? Do I ignore today's messages? Do I have protective devices to help me through the shocks in my life?

Smog check: an inspection which will determine if a vehicle emits pollution within a tolerable range. Getting a smog check corresponds to checking your nasal passages or your lungs. You can ask yourself: Do I take cleansing breaths when I feel under pressure? Are my breathing systems working efficiently?

Solenoid: a relay in the starting system that will redirect power to the starter motor. This is the work of the adrenals in your body. Located above the kidneys, they produce the flight or flight response. A problem in this area indicates that you should ask yourself: Do I know when to start and stop? Can I stop mid-track and change direction if required?

Spark plugs: ignite the air / fuel mixture. They are your electrolytes, which help assimilate vitamins and minerals. Replacing your spark plugs require you to ask yourself: Am I aware of what I need for balance? Do I take vitamins or food supplements? Do I put good things in my body? Do I eat well enough to maintain good health?

Speedometer: indicates the rate of speed at which car is moving. It corresponds to your blood pressure and is a gauge of how fast you are moving through life. Difficulty with the speedometer indicates that you should ask yourself: Am I moving fast enough for my comfort zone? Am I pushing my limits? Am I moving too slowly? Am I too slow or too fast in my responses?

Stabilizer: keeps car from swaying and lurching on curves. It relates to your sense of grounding and being balanced. It is your ability to stay in control. A problem in this area indicates a good time to ask: Am I aware of what keeps me grounded and what throws me off balance? Do I know how to bring myself back into balance? Where in my life am I out of balance? Am I out of control? What do I need to do to feel more stable in my life?

Steering system: turns the front wheels. It corresponds to how you are in control of where you are going. In other words it is your goals, your aims, or your internal guidance system. If a problem occurs in this area of the car, you can ask yourself: Am I conscious of where I'm going with my life? Am I aware of what is needed while I'm traveling there? Am I sure I'm going the right direction? Do I set clear goals and then work to meet them? Do I go in one direction and then end up somewhere else and with no idea how I got there?

Suspension: a combination of shock absorbers and springs connected to the frame to provide a smooth ride over bumps. It represents balance within your nerves. Issues in this area can prompt these questions: Can I handle quick changes? Do I get frustrated when things don't go the way I've planned? On a scale of 1 – 10, how frustrated do I get when things do not go my way?

Tailgate: door at the back of an SUV or truck. It is your past history. When you need to repair or replace this part, you can ask yourself: Am I capable of controlling what I have to work on? Am I aware of what I may be losing or gaining by getting too close to someone ahead of me? Am I doing my job to the best of my ability? Have I been given more to do than I am capable of doing? Do I have things under control?

Taillights: indicators of a driver's intentions to vehicles behind the car. They are your vision of the past. A broken taillight requires you to ask yourself: Can I tell the difference between a past event and a present one? Am I capable of looking at the past, labeling it the past, and leaving it there?

Tailpipe: allows exhaust to be expelled from car. This part of the car refers to your elimination system or your colon. Difficulty in this area enables you to ask yourself: Am I capable of eliminating feelings, emotions, and processes that I no longer need? How efficiently do I let go of the past?

Thermostat: maintains proper temperature in the engine. It is your thyroid. A problem with the thermostat calls for you to ask yourself: Do I have difficulty getting started? Am I hyper-active or under-active? Can I sit still and be silent? Can I silence my "head chatter"? Am I a mover and a shaker? Am I the tortoise or the hare? Which is my normal pace? Am I a self-starter?

Tie rod: (See **steering system**) corresponds to your shoulders. You can ask yourself: Why can't I set a goal and move directly toward it? How do I block myself? What's creating my inability to follow where my head leads?

Timing belt / timing chain: synchronizes fuel delivery and exhaust with engine cycles. It represents your cyclic process, your own personal sense of timing. A problem here can be solved by asking yourself: Do I feel out of place or out of sync with time? Do I "just miss" experiences?

Tires: rubber tubes encircling a wheel that is filled with compressed air. Front tires relate to your hands. Rear tires refer to your feet. Tires keep you grounded; they represent your energy and balance. A flat tire means you are losing energy; it's time to rest up. Front tires deal with the future; rear tires deal with the past. A blow-out means you have lost your energy. Tires with no tread indicate that you are stressed in life. You don't have a good grip on life. Your understanding or your patience has worn down. Needing tire chains means that you need help with conditions that are not normal. They get you through the process if you are stuck, or they keep you from getting stuck. If they are not on right, they can cut the tire, so the point is that you are not doing anything about the message you are getting. You should take some time out and ask yourself: Do I need a better grip on life, especially with new thoughts or ideas? Having the tires aligned refers to your ability to move smoothly in a grounded way.

Torque converter: (See **clutch**) the "clutch" of an automatic transmission car. It couples the engine and the automatic transmission, and it represents the adrenals in the body. It is the part of you that gets you moving. It is your motivation, and more important, your ability to act on your motivation. Having to repair or replace the torque converter means it is time to ask yourself: What is stopping me? How can I motivate myself and follow through with my desires and goals? Where are my blocks? Do I understand my personal fears? Do I feel paralyzed to act? Do I just get so far and then stop?

Trailer hitch: connective device to allow the auto to haul a boat or trailer. It refers to your inclinations and to your obligatory nature (how obligated are you to carry other people's baggage with you or to carry your own baggage forward). You can ask yourself: Do I have a personality that can't let go of issues, baggage, or my past history? How light do I like to travel? If something goes wrong with the hitch, must I look at what I was carrying that I should have dropped? What am I carrying that really belongs to someone else?

Transaxle: (See **front-wheel drive**) an assembly consisting of a transmission and a differential (in front-wheel drive cars). It is your outlook to the future or to moving forward. It relates to your muscles. If you have difficulty here, you should ask yourself: Am I looking to the future? Am I holding onto the past? Does my past determine my future? Am I taking today and making it my future?

Transmission: sends the engine's power to the differential. The automatic transmission means that the gears are changed within the auto. Manual transmission means that the gears are changed by hand. The transmission relates to your emotions and to how you direct your energies emotionally. Are you aware of your emotions and what they are doing? If you have problems with the transmission, it's time to ask yourself: Do I act without thinking? Or do I plan my moves? If I drive an automatic car, I should be able to move automatically. Can I move from one thing to another smoothly? If I drive a manual, I should think and plan things more directly and consciously. If my automatic goes out, I haven't been moving automatically. Am I stuck in a rut?

Trunk: storage unit at rear of most cars. It refers to your hips, buttocks, stomach, or intestines. When there are issues regarding your trunk, you should ask yourself: How guilty am I about the past? Do I store too much of my past? What past issues should I release? Have I stored so much without processing it correctly that my system is toxic? Do I need to detoxify?

Trunk key: the key to unlock the memories of your past. If you lose your trunk key, you have lost your ability to access the storage place of your history.

Universal joint: a mechanical linkage which allows one spinning shaft to spin another to maintain control or stability while turning. This car part corresponds to your sense of equilibrium. It indicates difficulty with control and stability when making changes in your life. It relates to your past. A problem here should lead you to ask yourself: Can I maintain balance while changing my direction? Am I capable of change without pain or resistance? Do I make changes effortlessly?

Vocal warning device: plays recorded message to warn driver of conditions or problems. It is your inner voice, your conscience. It allows you to ask yourself: Do I listen to my intuitive side? Do I listen and act with my gut instinct? Do I trust and use my own intuition?

Voltage regulator: controls alternator current and output to and from the battery. It corresponds to your lymph system. If you have a repair or replacement in this area of the auto, you should probably ask yourself: Am I clear in my physical body? Am I constantly flushing the toxics out of my system? Do I feel overloaded with too much "stuff"?

Water: the fluid which runs through the cooling system. It is your consciousness or your awareness. Am I aware of how I'm using my thoughts and ideas? Am I taking in enough water or fluids?

Water pump: keeps the engine cool by circulating water through the engine, radiator, and heater core. It refers to your body's circulation or to difficulty controlling stress. It also refers to your bladder. If a problem occurs in this area, you should ask yourself: Am I aware when my body is becoming sluggish or non-productive? Am I capable of relaxing after a period of stress? How do I release stress? How do I deal with too much food or drink? Do I have elimination difficulties that I should deal with?

Weather stripping: seals the doors, windows, and trunk from the weather. It is your skin. If a problem occurs in this area, you should ask yourself: Do I have trouble finishing up petty details in my life? Do other people irritate me?

Wheels: form and give the tire shape and stability. Wheels relate to your personality and also how your attitude keeps the body aligned and adjusted. Malfunctions here indicate that you should ask yourself: What throws me out of balance? What or who can shift my energies so they are stable or unstable? Who or what makes me crazy?

Wheel cylinder: part of brake system that pushes a brake shoe against a brake drum to assist car in stopping. It is your wisdom to know when to stop or to know your boundaries. If you experience difficulties with the wheel cylinder, you should question: Am I wise enough to know when to stop? Am I wise enough to know where my boundaries are? Do I know how to slow down?

Windows: glass plates allowing exterior views. It is your view of the outer world. A broken window indicates that your view of the outer world is stuck or broken. When this occurs you can ask: How do I view the outer world? Is my view of the world clear? Is my view distorted or clouded? Do I tint my vision of the world to filter out harshness?

Windshield: protects the occupants of the car from road debris and allows view ahead or behind car. It relates to your perception or your view of the world. If it cracks, you have misinterpreted something in your perception of the world. The front window refers to your view of what's in front of you or your future. The rear window relates to your view of something in your past. These problems call for you to ask yourself: Is my vision clear for the future? Is my vision clear about the past? Am I capable of ascertaining correct distances in looking ahead or behind? Do I keep a clear view of my life?

Windshield wipers: keep the view clear when rain or other obstruction threatens. They are your awareness, and they help clarify your vision to help you see the future and take the fog away. When you replace your wipers or if a malfunction occurs, you can ask yourself: Am I capable of seeing clearly and understanding clearly? Do I see things as I wish they would be or as they really are?

Wiring: carries current to various parts of the car which need electricity to operate. Wiring relates to your nervous system. It's time to ask: Can I be objective about other people's views as well as my own? Can I see the pro and con? Can I at least relate to another point of view? Am I aware when my nerves are too frayed and not functioning properly?

About Nancy Tappe

Nancy Tappe has often described herself as "an ordinary person with an extraordinary talent." She is, indeed. Nancy's DNA heritage provided her with a combination of synesthesia and "the sight," as her Scottish grandmother might have said. Today scientists define her abilities as accessing a part of the brain that others cannot. Nancy is the owner of Colorology, an organization devoted to the study of the personality through the science of color. Nancy has devoted her life and career to the study of color, consciousness, awareness, and their applications to the human personality. She has a large clientele throughout the United States and in Switzerland. Today Nancy utilizes the magic of technology to disseminate her teachings and philosophy to a world-wide audience through a variety of books and websites. Check her out at www.nancyanntappe.com

About Kathy Altaras

Kathy Altaras is the owner of Aquila Media Productions, a small, niche-marketing publishing company specializing in non-fiction media products. She has known and worked with Nancy Tappe for over 35 years. A Navy wife of 33 years, she had two teaching careers, settling in with 12th grade and gifted students. Kathy likes exotic and remote travel, counting Mongolia, Central and South America, and Africa among her favorite places. For more information about other books and projects at Aquila Media Productions, see www.aquilamediaproductions.com.

Breinigsville, PA USA
13 April 2010
236078BV00001B/67/P